School of Systematic Theology

Book 3

God Speaks to the World:
The Doctrines of the Bible

A ministry of

Striving for Eternity Ministries

School of Systematic Theology
- Book 3 -

God Speaks to the World

- Lesson 1 – Revelation
- Lesson 2 – Inspiration
- Lesson 3 – Illumination and Authority
- Lesson 4 – Preservation and Canonicity
- Lesson 5 – The Apocrypha
- Lesson 6 – Preservation and Translation
- Lesson 7 – A Comparison of Translation
- Lesson 8 – Dispensationalism

A Ministry of
Striving for Eternity Ministries
www.StrivingForEternity.org

Lesson 1: Revelation

The term *revelation* refers to the "divine act of communicating to man what man otherwise would not know" (L. S. Chafer). It is God's self-disclosure to man.

There are two reasons why revelation was necessary:
1) God is, by His nature, inaccessible to man. (Isaiah 55:9)
2) Because of the fall, mankind broke fellowship with God. (Genesis 3:24)

This study will focus on the two broad categories into which all of our understanding of revelation falls: _____ revelation and _____ revelation.

I. NATURAL REVELATION

A. Definition
The revealing of God to man by means of _____ phenomena.

B. The Instruments of Natural Revelation
There are two instruments through which God reveals Himself to all of intelligent mankind:

1) Creation
   Scriptures
   Psalm 8:1-3   Psalm 19:1-6   Isaiah 40:12-14
   Acts 14:12-17   Romans 1:19-21

   Significance
   These verses teach that God is _____ revealed in nature. This revelation is universal and timeless. (Romans 1:19-21; Psalm 19:1-6).

2) Conscience
   Scriptures
   Romans 2:14-15; 9:1-2; 13:5   1 Peter 2:19
   1 Corinthians 8:7, 10, 12   2 Corinthians 1:12; 4:2

   Significance
   The conscience convinces a person of right and/or wrong.

C. The Purpose of Natural Revelation

1) To render man _____ (Romans 1:18-23)

2) To prepare for _____ revelation (Psalm 19:7-12)

D. The Limitation of Natural Revelation

The primary limitation of natural revelation is that it cannot inform for the purpose of _____. (Romans 10:13-17)

QUESTION: What if someone responds to the clear testimony of nature? Is that person condemned?

The principle of Scripture seems to indicate that if a person responds with devotion to all the revelation they have, God will provide for them further revelation. (Acts 10:1-8; 19:1-7)

II. SPECIAL REVELATION

A. Definition

The intervention into the natural course of things, which is supernatural both as to the _____ and the _____ (Chafer, vol. I, p.53)

Three significant characteristics of special revelation:

It is _____

It is _____

It is _____

B. The Instruments of Special Revelation

1) Miracles and Mighty Works of God – the intercession of supernatural or mighty events which were interpreted as works by God through His spokesmen

The rainbow and Noah
(Genesis 9:13-17)

The Red Sea and Moses
(Exodus 14:23-31)

The rain and Elijah
(1 Kings 17:1; 18:17)

2) Theophanies – a physical manifestation of God in some way. There are three types of these in Scripture:

   _____ theophanies (Exodus 13:21-22)

   _____ theophanies (Exodus 19:1-3)

   _____ theophanies (Genesis 16:7-14: 31:11-18; Joshua 5:13-15)

3) Dreams and Visions – God revealing truth while one slept (Daniel 7:1) or through a conscious, visual experience (Acts 10:9-16; cf. Acts 12:5-9)

4) Prophets – God's chosen spokesmen who would declare the message of the Lord.

   Forthtelling the _____ of God
   (Amos 3:7)

   Foretelling the _____ of God
   (2 Peter 1:21)

5) Incarnate Word (Jesus Christ) – the second Person of the Trinity (John 1:1) who became flesh (John 1:14) and declared God to mankind (John 1:18)

6) Scriptures – God's recorded and written revelation, including God's revelation of all of the above that He desired to be known throughout time.

Therefore, the Scriptures are God's self-disclosure and His will for mankind.

C. The Purpose of Special Revelation
Three primary purposes of special revelation:
1) To _____ mankind and _____ them back into a proper fellowship with Him (Psalm 19:7-8).

2) To _____ all those who know Him with His plan for them (2 Timothy 3:17; Hebrews 1:1).

3) To _____ Himself (2 Corinthians 1:20; Ephesians 3:21).

D. The Limitations of Special Revelation
Special revelation, particularly the Scriptures, is not universal in language, nor does it proclaim God timelessly as does natural revelation. Revelation must be in the _____ of the people and must be proclaimed by _____ in order for it to fulfill its purpose. (Romans 10:13-17)

THOUGHT QUESTIONS FOR LESSON 1

1. What are some examples of religions or beliefs that worship natural revelation? rather than recognizing it as God's self-disclosure?

2. An individual tells you that he lets his conscience be his guide. Explain to him why that is not a good idea, and explain to him the purpose of his conscience.

3. What is essential for events in history to be categorized as God's self-disclosure?

4. Read Joshua 5:13-15. How do we know that the revelation before Joshua was a physical manifestation of God?

5. What are two essential ingredients for God's special revelation to accomplish His purpose?

Lesson 2: Inspiration

In 2 Timothy 3:16, we read, "All Scripture is given by the inspiration of God." While many believers rightly defend this teaching of Scripture, very few are able to explain it. This lesson is designed to provide an understanding of the doctrine of inspiration.

I. THE DEFINITION OF INSPIRATION

A. Defining the Word (2 Timothy 3:16)
The word in the Greek is *theopneustos*, which is a compound of two words:
    theos = God   *pneustos* = breathing

In other words, the Scriptures are spoken by God or God-breathed.

B. Defining the Concept
The Holy Spirit superintended the biblical writers so that, while using their own _____, _____, and individual _____ they inscripturated God's Word without error in the original manuscripts.

Four truths help us understand this concepts:

1) Inspiration is ultimately _____. Our comprehension of it can only deal with the _____ and not the _____.

2) Inspiration is _____ to Scripture. Only Scripture can be said to be inspired by God.

3) It is the _____ and not the _____ that are inspired by God.

4) Authors were kept from both _____ as well as _____ when they inscripturated God's Word.

II. THE EXTENT OF INSPIRATION

A. Incorrect Views about the Extent of Inspiration

1) The Liberal View

    a) Those who are theologically liberal identify the Bible as merely a good _____ book. They believe that the Bible was "inspired" as any other good book.

    b) This view denies the _____ origin of Scripture.

2) The New Evangelical Views
   a) The _____ Theory
      The human writers of Scripture had intensified religious perception.

   b) The _____ Theory
      God inspired the thoughts and concepts of Scripture, but not the words of Scripture.

   c) The _____ Inspiration Theory
      Only those portions of Scripture dealing with _____ are inspired and inerrant.

3) The Neo-Orthodox View
   This view posits that the Bible _____ contains the Word of God whenever it speaks to you, i.e., makes an impact on you.

B. Correct Views on the Extent of Scripture
   1) Infallible
      Every _____ of the Bible is as God had intended each one to be.
      (2 Timothy 3:16; Psalm 19:7)

   2) Inerrant
      The Bible is without _____. This focuses on the necessary relation between the _____ of the words and the _____ of the message.

   3) Complete
      Some call this "plenary." This emphasizes that nothing needs to be _____ to the Bible and that nothing should be _____.

   4) Authoritative
      The Bible is God's _____ of One who has the right and power to command compliance in thought and deed upon His rational creatures.
      (Acts 17:30-31; Roman 14:12)

   5) Trustworthy
      All that God says in His Word is _____ and is either a present reality or shall come to pass.

   6) Eternal
      _____ and _____ will pass away before God's Word. The standards and precepts for character and morality will be in effect throughout eternity.

7) Sufficient
   The Bible is sufficient to meet _____ spiritual need of mankind. Specifically, it is sufficient for salvation and spiritual life.
   (2 Timothy 3:15-17; Romans 15:4)

III. THE DIFFICULTIES OF INSPIRATION

A. Inspiration and the Original Writings
Since we do not have the original writings, our acceptance of the inerrancy is ultimately based upon _____. However, this is not blind faith. It is faith based upon external evidence (the myriad of old manuscripts) and internal evidence.
(2 Timothy 3:16, 2 Peter 1:21)

B. Inspiration and Contradictions
Many claim contradictions in Scripture. While there are difficult places to understand, our difficulty in understanding them should not assume contradiction but a lack of evidence for reconciling the contradictions.
(2 Peter 3:16)

THOUGHT QUESTIONS FOR LESSON 2

1. Explain in your own words what the Bible means when it says that the Scriptures were "inspired by God."

2. What was inspired? The authors or the writings?

3. In discussing the validity of the Bible, a friend of yours says that she feels the Bible was inspired much like Shakespeare was inspired by nature or beauty. How would you respond?

4. A co-worker overheard you witness to someone and says to you that no one knows for certain that the Bible came from God. What would be your response to this person?

5. How should the believer look at apparent contradictions in the Scriptures?

Lesson 3:
Illumination and Authority

Having examined what revelation is and the source thereof, we now look to the effect of Scripture upon the mind of its reader i.e. the doctrines of illumination and authority.

I. ILLUMINATION

A. Definition
The present ministry of the Holy Spirit by which He enables mankind to understand and embrace the truths recorded in Scripture.
(Psalm 119:18-19, Luke 24:45, Ephesians 1:18)

Illumination is not only the idea of understanding the facts of Scripture, but it includes being influenced by the significance of the understood truths.

B. The Distinctions of Illumination, Revelation, Inspiration

1) The Distinction of Revelation
   Revelation is the _____ of truth by God.

2) The Distinction of Inspiration
   Inspiration is the _____ of truth by God through man.

3) The Distinction of Illumination
   Illumination is the _____ and acceptance by mankind of God's already revealed truths.

C. The Details of Illumination

1) The Spirit does not illuminate the Scriptures, but the _____.
   (2 Corinthians 4:4)

2) The Scriptures are infallible; people are not.
   It is the reader, not the Scriptures, with whom there is fault or lack of understanding.

3) The Spirit does not illuminate _____ people.
   Since it is a ministry of the Spirit in the life of a person, it must be true that the Spirit is in the person's life. This comes only by means of regeneration.
   (1 Corinthians 2:14, Romans 8:9, 2 Thessalonians 2:10-12)

4) Illumination is a _____ ministry.
It is made available to all believers and is dependent upon their efforts to _____ as well as _____ revelation.
(2 Timothy 2:15)

5) John 14:21 and 16:7-11 are promises of unique illumination for the _____.

These verses are not to be considered the normal understanding of illumination (unless there is someone alive who heard Jesus say the things He said on earth).

II. AUTHORITY

This doctrine is often forgotten in our understanding of the Bible. Since illumination is the understanding and acceptance of revealed truth, this doctrine necessarily follows.

A. Explanation of Authority

The God of the Scriptures has the right and power to command compliance in thought and deed on the part of His rational creation. Since God has provided revelation, recorded it through men into the Scriptures, and provides illumination of it, it only follows that we are obligated to comply with it.
(Acts 17:30-31)

B. Basis of Authority

1) The Role of the _____

   a) The Bible is profitable for doctrine, reproof, correction, and instruction in righteousness, that the man of God may be perfect, thoroughly furnished unto every good work
   (2 Timothy 3:16-17).

   b) According to 2 Peter 1:16-19, the Bible is more certain to determine truth than hearing the voice of God.

   c) The Bible was the deterrent and cure for the future error about which Paul prophesied to the Ephesian elders
   (Acts 20:32).

So the Bible is our ultimate basis of authority for determining what, and who, is right or wrong.

2) The Role of _____
   a) The Bible ("Moses and the prophets"), not experience ("though one rose from the dead"), is the determiner that Jesus said would convince men to believe the truth of the torment in hell.
   (Luke 16:27-31)

   b) Signs and wonders (experience) do NOT prove that an individual or the signs are from God
   (2 Thessalonians 2:9, Matthew 24:23-24)

   c) The performance of great religious works does not prove that the individual or the religious works are from God.
   (Matthew 7:22-23)

   d) It is _____ (not experience) that gives us evidence of things not seen.
   (Hebrews 11:1)

   e) Those considered blessed of God are those who have not _____ yet believed.
   (John 20:29)

Therefore, experience must always agree with _____ in order to be a valid indicator of truth.

3) The Role of _____
   The Bible makes it clear that our feelings and emotions are not an accurate source of truth because they are subjective, biased, and open to misleading and deception.

   a) Some are doomed to destruction because something _____ right to them.
   (Proverbs 14:12)

   b) Jeremiah pointed out that a man's heart is _____ above all things and desperately _____.
   (Jeremiah 17:9)

   c) One's heart can lead a person to error.
   (Hebrews 3:10)

d) A man's heart can lead a person to believe he/she is spiritual, when he/she is not.
(James 1:26)

e) Even the Apostle Paul realized his heart could be wrong in its judgments.
(1 Corinthians 4:3-5)

4. The Role of the _____
There is an important role every individual must diligently seek to fulfill in order to determine biblical beliefs and behavior and to correct unbiblical ones.

    a) The individual must be _____.
(1 Corinthians 2:15-16)

    b) The individual must be _____.
(Acts 18:24-28, Romans 12:1-2)

    c) The individual must be _____.
(Acts 17:11)

    d) The individual must be _____.
(2 Timothy 2:15)

The basis of our authority for life cannot rest in religious experiences or our own personal feelings. It must ultimately rest in God's revelation which was inscripturated through the inspiration of God and is illuminated in our minds by the Holy Spirit.

THOUGHT QUESTIONS FOR LESSON 3

1. Define in your own words these four biblical teachings:

   Revelation:

   Inspiration:

   Illumination:

   Authority:

2. What is necessary for the Holy Spirit to be able to illuminate Scripture? Give at least two answers.

3. A friend of yours tells you he believes tongues are right because he experienced it. Apart from the biblical teaching of this doctrine, what would be your instruction concerning the reliability of experience? Include Scriptures.

4. A friend of yours tells you that even though she knows her church does not have solid doctrine, she feels "good" when she goes there. What would you share with her about the place of emotions and authority? Include Scriptures.

Lesson 4: Preservation and Canonicity

The doctrine of preservation involves two primary areas of study as it relates to how our Bible was formulated: _____ and _____. This lesson will cover the general teaching of the doctrine of preservation and the specific teaching concerning canonicity. Lesson 6 will discuss how preservation relates to translations of the Scriptures.

I. PRESERVATION

A. The Statement about Preservation

"The Old Testament in Hebrew and the New Testament in Greek, being immediately inspired by God and, by His singular care and providence, kept pure in all ages, are therefore authentical; so in all controversies of religion, the church is to finally appeal to them."
(The Westminster Confession)

The preserving work of God refers to His _____ care through the work of men.

B. The Scriptural Teaching of Preservation

1) God has promised through His Word that Scripture will be _____.

   Psalm 119:89, 154   Matthew 5:18
   Isaiah 40:8   Luke 16:27

2) God has left men with the _____ of safeguarding His Word.

   Deuteronomy 4:2; 12:32   Jeremiah 26:2
   Proverbs 30:6   Revelation 22:18-19

The fact that God warned and commanded men about the purity of the Word indicates some responsibility of men. Because of these truths, modern day Christians may be fully confident that they possess the preserved Word of God.

II. CANONICITY

How did the Scriptures come to be limited to the books we now have? This is the issue of canonicity.

A. Definition

The word *canon* comes from the Greek word κανων and means "a rod for measuring." In reference to the Scriptures, the word describes the Scriptures as the measure for doctrine, practice, and the life of the church.

B. Determiners

The Old Testament leaves us with no real issues: During the first century, the church recognized the thirty-nine books that are presently in our Bible, for they had been accepted by Judaism.

But what were the criteria? There were basically four different rules for determining which writings may be said to be "canonical":

1) The writings must be _____ in origin (though not necessarily written by an apostle). This is a corroborating test, not a _____ test.

2) The writings must be _____ by the early Christian community.

3) The writings must demonstrate _____. This is the true test of canonicity. To determine *this*, three arguments must be met.
    a) Must be focused on the person and work of _____.

    b) Must be _____ either in precision of history, the depth of instruction, or degree of concentration on Jesus Christ.

    c) Must be _____ in content with the whole.
    With no other explanation as to why so much about Jesus' life survived all these years, it must have been something within the literature.

4) The writings must produce a positive _____ and _____ effect on the readers. Note the effect of the Koran and *Das Kapital* on their respective readers.

There has not been a substantial attempt to change the canon as we have it since A.D. 397 at the Council of Carthage.

C. Development

It is important to recognize that the role of the church in formulating the canon was _____ and not _____ what would constitute the New Testament. That is why the canon is a collection of authoritative writings and not an authoritative collection of writings.

Below is a survey of the early church's discovery of what we know as the New Testament.
1) New Testament recognition
- a) 1 Corinthians 14:37 - Paul recognized that what he wrote was authoritative.

- b) 1 Timothy 5:18 - The second half of the verse is a reference to the Gospel of Luke (10:7) and is classified in the text as Scripture.

- c) 2 Peter 3:15-16 - Peter identified Paul's writings as Scripture.

- d) Revelation 22:18-19 - John understood that his writing of Revelation was an authoritative book not to be tampered with by men. It is even possibly a reference to the entire Scriptures.

2) The Canon of Marcion, AD 140
Appealing to the desire of early Christians for limitations on the canon, Marcion published the first one (Luke plus 10 Pauline epistles). Unfortunately, Marcion was a heretic, and this forced the true church to begin to tackle the issue of what the authoritative writings were—and were not.

3) Persecution of Diocletian, AD 303
Because of his desire to be worshipped as the only god, Diocletian ordered all other sacred writings to be destroyed. This, once again, forced the church to determine which were and were not sacred and authoritative.

4) Eusebius and Constantine
With the "legalization" of Christianity in AD 313 by Constantine, Eusebius, a church historian, was asked to produce fifty copies of the New Testament. Further acknowledging the need to identify the authoritative Christian writings, he divided all the books that were purported to have apostolic authority into four categories:
- a) Universally Accepted
    These included _____ of the 27 books we presently have in the New Testament.

- b) Disputed Books
    1. Hebrews because of authorship
    2. James because of lack of a salvation message
    3. 2 Peter, 2 John, 3 John, and Revelation because of content
    4. Jude because of authorship and some content

c) Spurious Books
These books were written by the early church but without content and apostolic authority:
1. *The Shepherd of Hermas*
2. The *Didache*
3. Epistle of Barnabas

d) Heretical Books
Though these touted authorship from other writers of Scripture, they were, in fact, forgeries.

The books were those Origen said to be disputed among churchmen (AD 250). Other Christians in Alexandria and he interpreted the Bible allegorically and typically rather than literally. This led Origen and others toward some very strange doctrine (e.g. unpurged souls being brought back to earth in different bodies).

5) Athanasius and the Festal Letter of AD 365
In this letter, Athanasius, a church leader, limited the New Testament to 27 books (those we have now) and forbade the *Didache* and *The Shepherd of Hermas* as authoritative writings.

6) The Council of Carthage, AD 397
This Council formulated the following statement:
> ". . . Nothing except the canonical Scriptures be read in the church under the name of Divine Scripture. . . Of the New Testament, the four gospels, Acts, thirteen epistles of St. Paul, the epistle of the same to the Hebrews, Peter (2), John (3), James, Jude, Apocalypse. . ."

THOUGHT QUESTIONS FOR LESSON 4

1. Your Roman Catholic friend suggests that the Roman Catholic Church is the one true church because it gave us the Bible. What would you say to him?

2. An atheist says that the Bible cannot be trusted because it was written by men. How would you respond?

3. Someone remarks that the Bible has been changed so much over time that we cannot know what it originally said. How would you approach her conclusion?

Lesson 5:
The Apocrypha

Many brought up in the Roman Catholic Church are familiar with the Catholic translations of the Bible, some of which are good translations (i.e. The Douay Version). However, because the Douay and other translations mingle the Apocrypha into the Old Testament, we must question whether these books are part of the canon. If not, how did they find their way into the Catholic translations— and some of the Protestant ones?

I. WHAT IS THE APOCRYPHA?

The Apocrypha of the Old Testament is a group of 13-15 books (depending on who named and included them) that were written from 300 BC to AD 100. Below is a description of the extra books and how they came to be accepted by some.

A. The Books
The books included in the Apocrypha generally fall into five descriptive categories:
---Note: This section has been adapted from Doug Bookman's notes on Bibliology. ---

    1) Wisdom Literature

        a) The Wisdom of Solomon

        A treatise in praise of righteousness and wisdom and in denunciation of iniquity and idolatry, written by an Alexandrian Jew around _____ BC.

        b) Ecclesiasticus (The Wisdom of Jesus, Son of Sirach)

        A long ethical treatise which contains general instruction in morality and practical godliness. It follows the model of _____.

    2) Historical Literature

        a) I Esdras (Greek for "Ezra")

        A free narrative of the last days of Judah, the exile in Babylon, and the return. Long sections of this work are wholly fabulous.

        b) I Maccabees

        A valuable historical narrative which covers about _____ years of the Maccabean Wars and the noble Jewish struggle for independence.

        c) II Maccabees

        A work that covers a portion of the period of I Maccabees but is very _____ and almost _____.

3) Religious Romance
   a) Tobit
      A moral fiction written around _____ BC. It is the tale of a pious Nephtalite, Tobit, with a son named Tobias. Tobias is directed by an angel to marry a widow; she is yet a virgin, though married before to seven men who were killed by a demon named Asmodeus on the day of their marriage. Tobias escapes death by burning the innards of a fish, the smoke of which exorcised the demon. Tobias then healed his father's blindness by anointing his eyes with the gall of the fish.

   b) Judith
      A tale of a rich, beautiful Jewish widow, who through seduction and deceit beguiled a Babylonian general and thus saved her own city from destruction. This book is patently _____ as it teaches that

      Judith's end justified the treachery she employed. This book was written about _____ BC.

4) Prophetic Literature
   a) Baruch (with the Epistle of Jeremiah)
      A book of prayers and confessions of Jews from the days of _____ along with the promises of restoration supposedly made by Baruch, imitating the style of Jeremiah.

   b) II Esdras
      An apocalyptic religious treatise, recording _____ revelations supposedly given to Ezra in Babylon.

5) Legendary Additions
   a) Prayer of Manasseh
      A deeply penitent (supposed) prayer of Manasseh, the wicked king of Judah who was carried to Babylon and there repented.

   b) The Rest of Esther
      Visions, letters, and prayers supposedly to be interjected in various parts of the book of _____ . These intend to explain perceived difficulties with the canonical book of Esther (additions included in RCC edition of Esther).

   c) Song of the Three Hebrew Children
      A petition of Azariah, an account of the deliverance along with a psalm of praise. This is included after _____ chapter 3.

d) The History of Susanna
      A tale of a rich Jewess in Babylon who is exonerated of the charges of two immoral men by the wisdom of _____.

   3) Bel and the Dragon
      A spurious, quite melodramatic tale of how _____ destroyed two objects of Babylonian worship, Bel and a dragon, and how Daniel escapes the lion's den.

B. The Background
   1) The _____ rejected these Apocryphal books as part of the canon because they were written after 400 BC (beyond the time when the canon was closed until the coming of the Messiah).

   2) Some of the manuscripts of the Septuagint (Greek translation of the Old Testament) included the Apocryphal books as an addendum to the Old Testament.

   3) At the Council of Carthage (AD 397), they were included in the OT books that could be read in the church, though not accepted as Scripture.

   4) It was for this reason that Jerome reluctantly included them in his Latin translation, the Vulgate.

   5) Since they were included in the Vulgate, the _____ _____ accepted them as Scripture.

   6) About 1540, Martin Luther translated the Apocrypha into German but set them apart from Scripture. He wrote in his forward that they were not to be regarded as sacred Scripture even though they could be read with profit.

   7) The Roman Catholic Church quickly responded, and at the Council of _____ (1546), they declared all the Apocrypha (except 1 and 2 Esdras and the Prayer of Manasseh) as canonical. They further declared every person who rejected these books to be anathema.

II. WHY DO WE REJECT THE APOCRYPHA AS CANON?

A. The Apocrypha were neither a part of the _____ canon nor ever accepted by the _____ as Scripture.

B. Although the Apocrypha was included in the Septuagint, it was an addendum, not to be accepted as Scripture.

C. Neither _____ nor the _____ ever quoted from one of these fourteen books.

D. The _____ of these books is very questionable.
   1) They abound in historical and geographic inaccuracies and anachronisms (not in proper time of history).
      a) 2 Esdras 6:42ff
      b) Much of 2 Maccabees

   2) They teach doctrines which are false practices and false practices which are at variance with inspired Scripture.
      a) 2 Maccabees 12:39-45
      b) Judith

   3) They resort to literary types and display an artificiality of subject matter contrary to the rest of canon.
      a) Tobit
      b) 2 Maccabees
      c) 2 Esdras

   4) They lack the distinctive elements which typify the rest of canon.
      a) The Wisdom of Solomon
      b) Ecclesiasticus
      c) Bel and the Dragon

E. They were rejected by virtually all of Christendom until the Council of Trent in 1546.

Lesson 6:
Preservation and Translation

The doctrine of preservation involves two primary areas of study that relate to how we obtained our Bible the way it is: _____ and _____. This lesson addresses how God preserved His Word through the translations. We will note the two most significant ancient translations, the three families of Greek translations that are the basis for our translations, the Textus Receptus, and then note some of the earliest English translations.

I. ANCIENT TRANSLATIONS
A. The Septuagint (LXX)
1) This is a translation of the _____ into the _____.

2) The translation was done in the _____ century BC.

3) Tradition teaches that 70 scholars translated the Old Testament separately, and when they came together, they found their manuscripts identical.

4) This was the translation from which Christ quoted.
Note: The fact that Christ willingly quoted from this translation when teaching about Scripture is a proof that our translations are also _____.

B. The Vulgate
1) It is a translation of the entire Bible into _____ by Jerome around AD 400.

2) This translation is the basis for the translations accepted by the Roman Catholic Church.

II. FAMILY OF GREEK TRANSLATIONS
This is a very detailed area of study concerning why there are variations among the best of the modern translations. While it is an important study, it needs to be understood that it only affects at the most a _____ of the Bible and **does not** affect any major doctrine of Scripture. There are basically _____ families of manuscripts.

A. The Alexandrian Manuscripts
1) These manuscripts make up our _____ family of Greek texts that the modern translations are based upon.
2) The New American Standard Bible is primarily based upon this family.

B. The Byzantine Manuscripts

1) These manuscripts were reproduced around AD 1000 and are very reliable.

2) The Byzantine family makes up about 80-90 percent of our ancient manuscripts. The dominance of the Byzantine Empire, which would only reproduce Byzantine text-types, is the reason for our high percentage of these texts.

3) This is the foundation for the King James Version of the Bible.

4) This is considered the better family of text for a number of reasons:
   a) The overwhelming majority of ancient manuscript witnesses are from the Byzantine family of texts.

   b) F. H. A. Scrivener, a noted textual critic of the 1800s, states, ". . . The worse corruptions to which the New Testament has ever been subjected originated within a hundred years after it was composed. . ."

   c) The Alexandrian texts place the weight of their acceptance primarily on two manuscripts, the Codex Vaticanus and the Codex Sinaticus, both of which do not always agree with one another.

   d) The Codex Sinaticus also omits a great deal of Scripture found in other significant manuscripts.

   e) The Eastern Christians (i.e. Origen) were spiritualists in their interpretation of Scripture, and it was in this area of Christianity that the greatest amount of doubt was cast upon some of the books of the Bible.

   f) The witness of the older manuscripts must have drawn from a comparison of early manuscripts, which gave the scribes of the newer manuscripts the opportunity to examine critically the flaws of the older manuscripts.

C. The Western Manuscripts

1) These are very few in number and the most unreliable of the family of manuscripts.

2) This family was the primary basis for the Douay Version of the Bible (Roman Catholic Church).

III. THE TEXTUS RECEPTUS

Many who claim the King James Version as the only reliable version place their belief in the reliability of the Textus Receptus.

A. It was written about AD 1515, compiled by Erasmus.

B. This was (rushed to be) the first New Testament printed on the new Gutenberg Press.

C. The text was compiled by Erasmus from representative families of translations and the Latin Vulgate.

D. The original Textus Receptus was full of typographical errors and included words that did not even exist in the Greek (thus *NOT* inspired, as some believe).

E. His original edition omitted 1 John 5:7. Because of the outrage from those accepting the Latin Vulgate, even though he did not find the verse in ANY manuscript, he included it to keep peace in 1532.

The revised Textus Receptus is largely supported by the Byzantine manuscripts and the Majority Text, the latter two correcting any weak manuscript support.
(e.g., 1 John 5:7)

IV. EARLY ENGLISH TRANSLATIONS

A. The Wycliffe Translation

    1) John Wycliffe's translation was completed in 1382.

    2) This was not a translation from the Greek and Hebrew, but a translation from the _____.

    3) For his efforts in translating the Bible into the language of the people, he suffered persecution.

B. The Tyndale Translation

    1) William Tyndale's translation was completed in 1526.

    2) This translation was prepared from the Greek manuscripts.

C. The Great Bible

    1) This was translated in 1539.

    2) The Great Bible was the first authorized translation into English.

D. The Geneva Bible

    1) Marion exiles in Geneva translated this version in 1539.

    2) This was the Bible of the Puritans.

Lesson 7:
A Comparison of Translations

There are six English translations used by churches and Christians. In this study, we will examine the history of these texts, their strengths, and their weaknesses.

I. THE KING JAMES VERSION (KJV)
Also known as the Authorized Version (AV)

A. Its History
1) Because of the variability of independent versions, the Puritans petitioned King James I in 1603 to find a solution. This resulted in a conference at Hampton Court in 1604. One statement from this conference:
   > "That a translation be made of the whole Bible, as consonant as can be to the original Hebrew and Greek; and this to be set out and printed, without any marginal notes, and only to be used in all churches of England in time of divine service."

2) Work began in 1607, and the version was complete in 1611. Fifty men made up six panels of translators. Three panels worked on the Old Testament, two panels on the New Testament, and one panel on the Apocrypha.

3) In 1611, three revisions were accomplished. Because of their respective renderings of Ruth 3:15, the first was known as the "he" Bible, and the last two were called the "she" Bibles.

4) The revisions that make up our King James Version were effected at Cambridge in 1762 and at Oxford in 1769 in order to modernize the language of the previous Authorized Versions.

B. Its Features
1) A very literal and reliable translation, based upon the _____ family of manuscripts and the Majority Text.

2) Its only drawback is the use of archaic and obsolete words, making its reading difficult at times for the modern reader.
   a) Pronouns – _____

   b) Words – _____

3) Some of the theology of its translators is evident in their translation:
    a) Choice to not translate _____.

    b) Translation of Acts 2:47 – "And the Lord added to the church daily such as should be saved."

II. THE REVISED STANDARD VERSION (RSV)

A. Its History
1) "The Revised Standard Version of the Bible is an authorized revision of the American Standard Version, published in 1901, which was a revision of the King James Version, published in 1611" (Preface, p. iii).

2) This text was based on the Masoretic (6th to 9th century AD) in the Old Testament and combined families in the New Testament.

3) Thirty-two scholars completed the entire Revised Standard Version in 1952.

B. Its Features
1) This text has often come into question for its consistent bent toward _____ theology.
    a) Colossians 1:14 – "[T]hrough the blood" is omitted (so also in the NASB and the NIV).

    b) Acts 8:37 – The complete verse is omitted (placed in the margin of the NIV).

    c) Isaiah 7:14 – "[V]irgin" is translated as "young woman" ("virgin" placed in margin).

2) The RSV is basically a literal translation, though often not used by conservative evangelicals because of concerns over these liberal tendencies.

III. NEW AMERICAN STANDARD BIBLE (NASB)

A. Its History
1) This translation was realized because of the perceived need to incorporate recent textual discoveries and rendering it into English more modern than the 1901 American Standard Version.

2) The editorial team completed this version in 1971.

B. Its Features

1) "When it was felt that the word-for-word literalness was unacceptable to the modern reader, a change was made in the direction of a more current English idiom" (Preface to NASB).

2) While it is idiomatic, it still may be considered a _____ translation.

3) The NASB is based primarily on the New Testament work of the Nestle's *Novum Testamentum* text (based on the Alexandrian family of manuscripts).

4) Because of its exclusive reliance on the fewer and older manuscripts, it often omits or notes omissions of various texts in its margin (e.g. Colossians 1:14).

IV. THE NEW INTERNATIONAL VERSION (NIV)

A. Its History

1) This version was developed by establishing a series of three committees:
   a) The translators' translation of the Bible books provides a basis.

   b) These translations were then reviewed by one of the Intermediate Editorial Committees for revision.

   c) From there it went to the General Editorial Committee for further revisions.

   d) The Committee on Bible Translation was the final revision.

2) The actual work on the NIV was completed in 1978.

B. Its Features

1) While asserting to have drawn from all families of the Greek text, the translators' desire for a modern English translation resulted in the NIV being a _____ translation and not a very literal translation.

2) It eliminates a large amount of verses from the actual text
   Matthew 17:21, 18:11, 23:14   Mark 7:16; 9:44, 46; 11:26; 15:28
   Luke 17:36, 23:17   John 5:3-4
   Acts 8:3, 15:34, 24:7, 28:29 Romans 16:24

   This does not include a number of portions from other verses.

3) Some of its translations are weak (e.g. "he" instead of "God" in 1 Timothy 3:16).

4) As a translation, it too often interprets (e.g. 1 Samuel 15:33 "and Samuel put Agag to death"; 1 Peter 1:2 "for obedience to Jesus Christ").

5) This translation may be helpful in Bible study, but it must be recognized as a free translation and not a literal translation.

V. THE NEW KING JAMES VERSION (NKJV)
A. Its History
1) The Preface authors of the 1611 Authorized Version stated that the purpose was not "to make a new translation...but to make a good one better." They spoke of The Bishop's Bible. The New King James editors used the above statement to refer to their new translation.

2) For the Old Testament, they drew from a number of ancient Hebrew texts, the Septuagint, the Vulgate, and relevant portions from the Dead Sea Scrolls.

3) The New Testament was based upon the Byzantine texts with references made to various manuscripts discovered since the Authorized Version was completed.

4) This version was completed in 1982.

B. Its Features
1) Should there be differences in the manuscript witness, the NKJV includes variant readings in the margins of the NU (Nestle's Greek) and the M (Majority Text).

2) The NKJV also includes the fullness of the King James Version and the literal translating that characterized the KJV.

3) The NKJV eliminates the archaic or obsolete words and replaces them with accurately translated alternatives.

VI. The English Standard Version (ESV)
A. History
1) The ESV has grown out of the Tyndale–King James legacy. With the 1971 RSV text as its starting point, the ESV had a fourteen-member Translation Oversight Committee that benefited from the work of fifty biblical experts.

2) The translators drew mostly from the Masoretic Text for much of the Hebrew. In some cases, they looked to the Dead Sea Scrolls, the Septuagint, the Samaritan Pentateuch, and other sources.

3) The Greek text was based mostly on the 1993 editions of the Greek New Testament (4th corrected edition) published by United Bible Societies and the *Novum Testamentum Graece* (27th edition) edited by Nestle and Aland. The translators used other Greek manuscripts to help with difficult passages, but only sparingly.

B. Features

1) The ESV is an "essentially literal" translation and seeks to be transparent to the original text.

2) Like the NKJV, it updates the archaic or obsolete wording of the KJV for more accurate understanding. Like the KJV, there are language study tools for a word-for-word rendering of the original text.

Lesson 8: Dispensationalism

Among evangelicals, there are generally two approaches to interpreting the Scriptures: covenant theology and dispensational theology. The two may be contrasted in this way:

COVENANT THEOLOGY	DISPENSATIONAL THEOLOGY
Infant baptism	Believer's baptism
No distinction between Israel & church	Distinction between Israel & church
Generally amillennial	Consistently premillennial

A dispensational approach to Scripture is not an attempt to place a manmade approach on interpretation; it is a way to describe the _____ revelation of God and its outworking and application for our lives today. For example, why do we not offer sacrifices on an altar? A dispensational approach understands that work as a responsibility of Israel, no longer necessary today since Jesus Christ fulfilled that picture in the progression of God's plan.

In this lesson, we will draw out a definition of dispensationalism, the essentials of a dispensational theology, and a survey of each dispensation.

I. A DEFINITION OF DISPENSATIONALISM

A. The Greek Term
The Greek term, which is translated as "dispensation," is the word *oikonomia*. The basic meaning of this word is _____ of someone else's property. (Luke 16:2-4)

B. The Term Applied to Dispensationalism
Dispensationalism is the "distinguishable economy in the outworking of God's program" (Ryrie). These economies each include the following:

1) The giving of new _____

2) A change in the God-man _____

3) For mankind, a corresponding _____

II. THE ESSENTIALS OF DISPENSATIONALISM

There are three essential truths that distinguish dispensationalism from other approaches to Scripture:

A. It recognizes and maintains a distinction between _____ and the _____.

B. It will consistently employ a _____ (or literal) interpretation of the Scriptures.

C. It regards the underlying purpose of God as being for His _____ and not simply for the redemption of mankind (doxological rather than soteriological).

III. A SURVEY OF DISPENSATIONS

By surveying these dispensations, we are analyzing the history of God's plan with regard to mankind. Seven dispensations are generally accepted.

A. The Dispensation of _____

    1) The Time - Creation through the Fall

    2) The Revelation and Responsibility
        a) Replenish the earth (Genesis 1:28).
        b) Subdue the earth (Genesis 1:28).
        c) Exercise dominion over the animals (Genesis 1:28).
        d) Dress and keep the garden (Genesis 2:16).
        e) Eat vegetables (Genesis 1:29-30).
        f) Abstain from fruit of "tree of knowledge of good and evil" (Genesis 2:1-17).

    3) The Failure - Knowingly Partook of the Tree

    4) The Judgment
        a) Curse upon mankind, animals, and earth (Genesis 3:14-19).
        b) Sin and death entered the world (Romans 5:12).
        c) Adam and Eve were expelled from the garden (Genesis 3:22-24).

B. The Dispensation of _____

1) The Time – The Fall to the Flood

2) The Revelation and Responsibility
   a) Believe in God's promised Redeemer (Genesis 3:15).
   b) Demand for blood sacrifice (Genesis 4).

3) The Failure
   a) Cain's rebellion and murder
   b) The rise of a wicked and violent society

4) The Judgment - The Flood

C. The Dispensation of _____

1) The Time – The Flood to the Fall of Abraham

2) The Revelation and Responsibility
The new revelation was the _____ covenant, which included these four features:
   a) Fear of man placed within animals (Genesis 9:21)
   b) Permission to eat meat (Genesis 9:3)
   c) Capital punishment for murder (Genesis 9:6)
   d) God's promise never to destroy the earth by water again (Genesis 9:8-17).

3) The Failure
   a) The drunkenness of Noah (Genesis 9:2)
   b) Rebellion against God's desire for mankind to spread throughout the earth (Genesis 11:1-9)

4) The Judgment - Dividing of Languages and Races

D. The Dispensation of _____

1) The Time – The Call of Abraham to the Giving of the Law

2) The Revelation and Responsibility
The new revelation was the _____ covenant, which included these three features:
   a) A seed - Abraham was to be the father of a great nation.
   b) A land - Promised with carefully specified borders (Genesis 15:18).
   c) A blessing - Promised to all the earth through Abraham (Genesis 12:1-3).

3) The Failure - Abraham's Seed (Israel) Remaining in Egypt

4) The Judgment - Bondage in Egypt (Exodus 1:8-14)

E. The Dispensation of _____

1) The Time – The Giving of Law at Mt. Sinai to Pentecost (Acts 2:1-4)

2) The Revelation and Responsibility
The Mosaic Law was the new revelation of God and the responsibility of mankind. The Mosaic Law included the following three elements:
   a) The _____ Element
      The social and legal relationships of Israel

   b) The _____ Element
      The rituals, dress, and demands of the Levitical religious system

   c) The _____ Element
      Legislation of the moral will of God (i.e. the Ten Commandments)

3) The Failure
   a) Israel failed in the keeping of the law.
   b) Israel rejected the One who came to fulfill the law (Romans 10:1-3).

4) The Judgment
   a) Temporary rejection of Israel (Matthew 21:43)
   b) Destruction of Jerusalem, AD 70 (Luke 21:20-24)

F. The Dispensation of the _____

1) The Time - Pentecost to the Second Coming of Christ

2) The Revelation and Responsibilities
   a) To receive by faith the offering of Jesus Christ, thus being indwelt by the Holy Spirit
   b) To unite with a local church of Bible-believers (1 Timothy 3:14-16)
   c) To fulfill Jesus' Great Commission (Matthew 28:19-20)

3) The Failure
Rejection of the truth of Scripture (1 Timothy 4:1-3) resulting in the great apostasy of the tribulation period (2 Thessalonians 2:1-12)

4) The Judgment
   a) Eternal damnation for rejecting Christ
   b) The tribulation period

G. The Dispensation of the _____ of God

    1) The Time – The Second Coming of Christ to the Final Rebellion of Satan

    2) The Revelation and Responsibility
    The Millennial Kingdom will be the physical reign of Christ on the earth, meting out justice in connection with. . .
        a) The Social Dimension of the Kingdom (Isaiah 2:4)
        b) The Political Dimension of the Kingdom (Isaiah 32:1)
        c) The Moral Dimension of the Kingdom (Isaiah 32:5)
        d) The Physical Dimension of the Kingdom (Isaiah 351)
        e) The Religious Dimension of the Kingdom (Isaiah 40-48)

    3) The Failure
    Satan is loosed and leads a rebellion against God and His Christ with an unnumbered multitude (Revelation 20:9-10).

    4) The Judgment – Fire from Heaven (Revelation 20:9-10)
    This dispensation leads into the _____.

It must be noted that through all the dispensations from the Fall onward, the means of salvation transcends dispensational truth. Note the following truths about salvation in the plan of God:
    a) The BASIS at all times - The death of Christ
    b) The ACCOMPLISHING of salvation all times - God's grace
    c) The OBJECT of that faith in every dispensation - God's Word
    d) The CONTENT of that faith - Differs from each dispensation

THOUGHT QUESTIONS FOR LESSON 8

1. Some like to call the dispensation of the church the "Age of Grace." Why would this not be a good title?

2. A covenant theologian believes that he must sprinkle babies because baptism took the place of Old Testament circumcision. What is the primary challenge to this interpretation? How does a dispensationalist's interpretation differ?

3. Why is it important to understand the purpose of God as doxological (the goal being His glory) rather than soteriological (the goal being redemption)?

4. A friend of yours disagrees with dispensationalism, saying that it divides up the Bible too much. How would you respond to this criticism?

BIBLIOGRAPHY

Bruce, F. F. The Canon of Scripture. Downers Grove, IL: Inter Varsity Press, 1988.

Carson, D.A. The King James Debate. Grand Rapids: Baker Book House, 1979.

Comfort, Philip Wesley (ed.) The Origin of the Bible. Wheaton, IL: Tyndale House Publishers, 1992.

Ewert, David. From Ancient Tablets to Modern Translations. Grand Rapids: Zondervan Publishers, 1983.

Geisler, Norman L. (ed.) Inerrancy. Grand Rapids: Zondervan Publishers, 1980.

Hannah, John D. (ed.) Inerrancy and the Church. Chicago: Moody Press, 1984.

Henry, Carl F. H. God, Revelation, and Authority. Waco, TX: Word Book Publisher, 1977.

Lewis, Gordon and Bruce Demarest (ed.). Challenges to Inerrancy. Chicago: Moody Press, 1984.

MacArthur, John F. Why I Trust the Bible. Wheaton, Il: Victor Books, 1983.

Metzger, Bruce M. The Text of the New Testament. New York: Oxford University Press, 1980.

Pickering, Wilbur. The Identity of the New Testament Text. Nashville: Nelson Publishers, 1977.

Ryrie, Charles C. What You Should Know about Inerrancy. Chicago: Moody Press, 1981.

Tan, Paul Lee. Literal Interpretation of the Bible. Rockville, MD: Assurance Publishers, 1978.

Warfield, B. B. The Inspiration and Authority of the Bible (edited by Samuel Craig). Grand Rapids: Baker Book House, 1948.